WORDS AFTER WAKING

Copyright © 2025 by Colton Hamilton

All rights reserved. No part of this book may be reproduced, distributed, or transmitted in any form or by any means, including photocopying, recording, or other electronic or mechanical methods, without the prior written permission of the publisher, except in the case of brief quotations embodied in critical reviews and certain other noncommercial uses permitted by copyright law.

For permission requests, contact: info@hamiltonnexus.com

ISBN: 979-8-218-62813-0

First Edition

Published by Hamilton Nexus, LLC

www.hamiltonnexus.com

To Herald:

You are the best of our Warriors
You are the best of our Kings.
You are the best of our Poets, the lovers who dream.
You are the best of our Magic, with words thought out well.
Your truest words cast the most powerful spell

Table of Contents

INTRODUCTION viii

Part I .... *x*

   WORD MAGIC 2

   THE PROCESS TO PATRIARCH 4

   THE FINAL GOODBYE 8

   PEOPLE 12

   NECESSARY HEARTACHE 14

Part II *16*

   HARMONIZING POWER 18

   LIFE'S CAPTAINS 20

   UNTITLED #1 24

   UNCOMFORTABLE TRUTHS 26

Part III *28*

   THE FIRST LOOK 30

   THUNDERSTORMS 34

   INTERIM 38

   MOTHER'S LOVE 42

   UNTITLED #2 44

   DEAR YIN 46

Part IV *50*

   BE THE GUY 52

   FAMILY MEETING 56

      UNTITLED #3 58

THE PERFECT SHOE	60
Part V	*62*
HEART BEATS	64
YONI	66
UNTITLED #4	68
THE LIFE WE EARNED	70
Part VI	*74*
ABUNDANCE PRAYER	76
THE ITCH TO BE WEALTHY	78
UNTITLED #5	80
UNTITLED #6	82
NEW EARTH FRONTIER	84
ACKNOWLEDGMENTS	98
ABOUT THE AUTHOR	100

INTRODUCTION

What is something you never saw yourself doing, but eventually gravitated to? For me, this is poetry.

When I wrote my first poem, I never intended to publish a book. I grew into the confidence to do this slowly. My poetry began as a way for me to simply organize my thoughts; to understand myself and how I truly felt about whatever happened to be on my mind. Poetry is my way of processing life, one meditation at a time.

Therefore, I only write when I have something to say, so each poem you'll find is the result of life's happenings and my internal dialogue in response to such things.

It's a given that we are all individuals, and no two lives are the same, but I also recognize that I am human–as we all are. The emotions I work through in these pages are not exclusive to myself–they are thoughts and feelings that all humans have the capacity to experience, and most likely do, to some degree. It's like in grade school or business meetings: if one person has a question, there are likely other people thinking the same thing or something similar. This is why I have compiled this collection.

Feel free to skip around this book and read any poems that appeal to you in the moment. I have organized these works in (roughly) chronological order of their writing, though it is not necessarily meant to be read in such fashion.

But, if you do read this collection from the first page to last, you will witness my journey of the two years past. You'll see me process heartbreak and fall in love. You'll find my thoughts on freedom and rising above the noise of distractions and mindless chatter so I can focus on the true meaning of what really matters. You'll hear me give advice to a friend during his own time of struggle and my thoughts about family where conflicts can muddle.

This collection kind of has it all. It includes both quick ideas of digestible chunks and longer free verse narratives that depict glimpses of my story–glimpses I am finally ready to share.

For me, writing these poems was only half of my process. The other half was to own who I was, who I found myself to be. To do this, I realized I needed to speak my truth out loud, and not just when I was alone. To truly own who I was, and maybe this is the case for us all, I needed to speak my truth directly to another person. After all, this is how we know we aren't crazy or off kilter.

So, I did just that. I shared my first poem with a close friend. Then my next. They resonated with my work; and frankly, they were impressed that I wrote such pieces. And to be completely transparent, I surprised myself too.

After all, I am just a traditional red-blooded all-American dude who grew up slamming beers and making jokes that were crude. It's amazing the kinds of shifts we can make in life–if we want to.

This is why I began reciting my poems at open mic nights. At a small café with an intimate and diverse crowd, I exposed my authenticity to complete strangers, much like yourself. I found they also resonated with my messages that carry an undertone of classical and traditional American values. The feedback from the crowds at these events has been consistently positive, indicating that traditional values are still felt in the world and possibly even longed for in this modern age.

I don't need or want to be the only Herald of the Change (yes, that is a Dune reference), but I can be one of them. And you can be too. My intention for you is the same as it is for the audiences to whom I recite my art: take what serves you and leave what doesn't. If you like the poems, that's good. If you resonate with them, great! If you take a piece of them with you, I would be truly honored. In any case, I thank you for your attention and I hope I leave you with something to ponder.

I do recommend reading one poem at a time. Sit with it. Feel it. Read it again. Analyze it if you wish. Use this book as you would a daily reader or morning meditation guide because the best things in life are savored, like sipping a fresh cup of morning coffee or an evening glass of fine wine. Consume your food and these words with patience and pay acute attention to the palette of flavors within these pages.

Happy reading! Or sad–it depends on the poem.

Part I

Be careful... words are a powerful magic.

That's why they call it Spelling.

(from Word Magic)

Part I

WORD MAGIC

May 2023

Be careful what you say and ask for.
Words are a powerful magic.

That's why they call it Spelling.

And if you don't believe me, go ahead…
Be reckless with your language
and you'll find yourself dwelling
in a pit of agony and despair
  with your misery swelling,
   and filling your cup to the brim
    with nothing that serves you,
    because you spoke on a whim
    without taking time to consider
     if what you said
     matches what you truly feel within.

On the other hand – If your spirit does match your speech,
you'll start to notice how each
of your spells begins to reach
the hearts of those you want to teach
  and creates a
  fortress for your soul
   that no evil
   can truly breach.

Speak true and live right.
This is how you protect yourself and the ones you love with divine daily light.

Words After Waking

Part I

THE PROCESS TO PATRIARCH

March 2023

It's the transience for me.
At least it used to be.

You see – I revere the temporary nature of the human
condition. Therefore,
>I unwittingly
>manifested
>past relationships
>ending in my vision.

Now – I knew each one would reveal a lesson
>for us both
>as we joined
>for the time being
>on life's journey of
>personal growth.

Each of them special – none of them the same.
>This thing called
>life can be a
>fun and
>cruel game.

But life is a process with many seasons.
And not that I need it, but life's changing season is my reason
to shed the framework of my younger self's vision.
Because if all things change, now too, does my mission.

The pricelessness of my proper spouse is now clear to me.

Words After Waking

In previous years, I stretched myself to full capacity.
I now know my limit.
My inner work has revealed what is sustainable
and what will inhibit
my forward progress
and fullest expression.

My highest self is not
>   the youth
>   blessed with
>   limitless options and
>   convenience.

My highest self is
>   the man who
>   reveres the
>   confines of my
>   individual genius.

Of course, I have high standards and like nice things,
but I don't need the
>   big house,
>   fast cars,
>   and bling.

My jewels and riches are found elsewhere.

And of all the things to learn from life and its unfolding, my favorite piece of wisdom has come in knowing to
>   save space
>   for silence.

Part I

I'll find my person that comfortably
shares this silent space.
I'll know what she feels like.
So I'll close my eyes and
forget about body and face.

At this point, life's trials and lessons make me feel like a modern-day sage.

Spirit, I feel you listening.
I'm ready to receive my mage.

The one I can laugh and share silence with so we can
       die young together
              at an old age.

Words After Waking

Part I

THE FINAL GOODBYE

April 2023

As we sit on this black sand beach and watch the
waves crash,
It becomes painfully clear that our
priorities clash.

Our journey began seven years prior when our love shined
bright. When I think of you, many things come to light.

For instance, I remember the road trip to Denver.
There was
> the ballgame,
> the joint,
> the river court night.

When I think of you, our time in Utah comes to mind.
I remember
> the mountains,
> the desert,
> and California coast

where I got to know your crazy family
> and saw where you learned
> to be so kind.

It hurts to think I'll have to
> finally,
> actually,
> leave you behind.

I remember the first and every time we truly
spoke of the future.

We discussed our visions and possibilities. We've meditated, contemplated, but just don't see our viable suture.

Some things are irreconcilable.

When we've parted ways over the years, it was always "See you later". Our connection kept up close at heart. It seems from this point forward,
someone new
> will be our
> fresh start.

It's precisely because we care too much to "just be friends" that if we can't share a life together, these periodic adventures must end.

We tried the friend thing.
It's clear that doesn't work.
We can lie to ourselves until we're blue in the face, but our deep connection will always lurk,
Waiting and ready to reveal itself
> as soon as it gets the chance.
> Like every time
> I take you in my hands.

You asked if I still feel it:
The energy that stirs inside when we touch.
My answer is a resounding yes,
> quite certainly,
> very much.

Some things are inextinguishable.

Part I

Many times, I was wrong.
Sometimes you were rude.
But I wouldn't change a thing.
It seems by tomorrow night,
        our beautiful story
        will conclude.

Before I fly back to the mainland, I'll kiss you.
And even if it goes unsaid, you'll know that
        I love you and
                I'll miss you.

This time, I fear, is our final goodbye.
The end of an era for you and I.

Words After Waking

Part I

PEOPLE

May 2023

When it comes to people:

Most are strangers.
Some are tribe.
Very few are truly familiar.
And only one is home.

To properly determine who plays which part,
I have found it's best to
        feel with your brain and
        think with your heart.

Words After Waking

Part I

NECESSARY HEARTACHE

May 2023

Rarely do we get what we want.
Sometimes we get what we need.
But we always get what we deserve.

I suppose hearts must break open so true love can find its way in. And the crazy part is that love breaks it in the first place.

There is a piece of advice that has brought me a good amount of heartache but saved me from much more. I'm sure. I'll share it with you now
>	in hopes that it helps you endure
>>		the waters of love
>	that can leave us unsure
>>		with the question of
>	"Do I leave it open or
>>		close this door?".

The advice is this:

Loving someone and building a life with them are two things that don't necessarily happen simultaneously.

It's one of the hardest things you'll ever do.
Stepping away from a love you want but know just simply
>	isn't true
>	or right.

Words After Waking

We have all seen what happens when couples
force their love and all they get
for their effort
        is years of
        obvious plight.
Not for me.
I deserve better.
I refuse to partake in that fight.

And this other piece of advice has helped me make the
tough, but right decisions:

That is, the heart is like an egg in the way that
if it breaks from an external force, life's process is halted.
If the heart breaks from an internal force, however, new life
and liberation is the manifestation – ultimately leaving you
exalted.

Like a weight off both our shoulders, because neither of us
are faulted for how our story turned out.

Our history doesn't leave much to mystery about the future.
I'm sure a life together
        would be
        just fine.
And even though I've always been a haven for you, It's time.
It's sad to say but,
        I'm not yours and
        you're not mine.
The answer is clear.
We must lay down our love,
for good this time, and part ways from here.

Part II

If I never experienced this full spectrum of passion and pain, I would not be what I am today...

(from Life's Captains)

Part II

HARMONIZING POWER

May 2023

Great men do not seek to lead.
They are called to it.

The greatest power is that which is bestowed without pursuit
        and acts for the well-being
        of the people it serves.
The applied commission of such a position
        is to establish a
        unified harmony of existence.
To see this to fruition,
        you'll need the strength of
        compassion and persistence.
And if indeed you are deemed worthy,
        it will not be without
        reason or rhyme.
Just bear in mind,
        this is a fine line to walk
        and a tough mountain to climb.
Prepare yourself,
        so you do not balk
        when it is your time.

Words After Waking

Part II

LIFE'S CAPTAINS

May 2023

Navigating these waters of the human experience takes skill.
The key to this is training the mind to
      be quiet and
      be still.
As with any practice, this takes time to master,
but if you keep at it,
      I'm confident
      that you will.

Like a heartbeat, life is full of
ebbs and flows,
      highs and lows,
stops and goes,
      and even some
zags and zigs
      with seasons
and reasons
      to either
            keep on climbing or
      drop the shovel and
stop the dig.

The only heartbeat without the necessary duality of
      joyful highs and
      sorrowful lows
      is a dead one –
      a flatline.
And that sure as hell ain't mine.

Words After Waking

And honestly, I hope it's not yours,
because that would be
>	a waste,
>	a shame,
>	or at the very least,
>	a bore.

If I never experienced the full spectrum of passion and pain,
I would not be what I am today:

The King of my realm who sits with my Dame.
And not to speak for her, but I'm sure she would agree. This
spectrum paints life's canvas full and
>	equips our quiver
>	with tools for you and me
>	to avoid the traps that,
>	all too often,

pull toward
spiritual malady.

But those who captain life's waters with
spiritual fortitude,
provide the solution
>	to dismiss delusion,
>	foster truth in a
>	world of illusion,
>>		and show others
>>		to see through a lens of
>>		high resolution.

Part II

Find these people and follow them.
Or better yet, become one yourself.
    And when you do finally master this,
    it cannot be undone.
And your people
will need your help.

Words After Waking

Part II

UNTITLED #1

Meet the pressure

and be what is called for.

Words After Waking

Part II

UNCOMFORTABLE TRUTHS

May 2023

Never apologize for shedding light on uncomfortable truths,
for this is an act of
>	courage,
>	compassion, and
>	clear sight.

Think about it like this:
>	If Truth is a woman,
>	it's best to address her soon
>	instead of letting her
>	fester in a room
>	sequestered to what
>	may look like her doom
>	to the untrained eye,
>	but if you suppress her
>	for too many moons,
>	she will rise
>	as a force formidable to
>	expose your lies
>	which, I'm sure you know,
>	amplifies your strife
>	and reveals the hidden carnage
>	that you refuse, until now,
>	to acknowledge in your own life.

Don't be reckless, address this.
When it comes to uncomfortable truths,
Face them head-on and save yourself the spiritual bruise.

Words After Waking

Part III

If connections are like candles, I've also learned

it's the slow burns that last.

(from The First Look)

Part III

THE FIRST LOOK

May 2023

You were wearing a
>   white button down, worn open,
>   crop top, and yellow pants.

You had clear quartz around your neck,
>   fire opal on your middle finger, and the
>   purest smile I've seen in all my days.

These are just a few things I remember
>   from the moment
>   you first captured my gaze.

But it's your eyes that I remember most clearly.

Without uttering a sound, we spoke,
>   and I witnessed
>   you hear me.

I recognized this ancient language
>   in the guise of
>   a passing glance.

I would regret it dearly if I let us part ways
>   without meeting you
>   and taking my chance.

I've learned to use my two eyes to look into the soul
>   and my third to see how it feels.

When I first saw this soul of yours, I recognized that
>   you are one who heals.

And in a world of illusions, it's refreshing to cross paths with
someone who seems to cherish what is Real.

As you gather your things and stand to leave,
I must say hello.

So, I take a moment.

And I breathe.

"Excuse me, Hi."

You reciprocate my interest with
> your smile and
> your hand.

As we exchange our first words, the energy in my chest
makes it difficult to stand still.
Apparently, I'm quite nervous,
and I wonder if you can tell.

I've been speaking with Spirit lately and asking for my
mage. For me, it's the water-bending nature girl,
who gets evermore beautiful
> with wisdom and
> with age.

And the best part is:
I believe I have finally found her
and I'm ready for this stage.

You know – if connections are like candles,
I've also learned it's the slow burns that last.

Part III

So, I'll take it slow and make it right.
And when our time does arrive,
>　it will be my honor
>　and spiritual delight.

Until then, go on, Butterfly.
>　Spread your wings
>　and take flight.

Strengthen your magic – I'll do the same.
And soon enough,
>　we'll join forces in
>　life's big crazy game.

Words After Waking

Part III

THUNDERSTORMS

June 2023

There is something about thunderstorms that I am drawn to.
There're a few things it could be, so let's think this through.

Maybe it's my chance to cry in disguise,
so nobody actually sees the tears
escape from my eyes.
I'll just credit the streams on my face to the
water from the skies.

But this is the obvious reason.
I feel there's something deeper.

For instance, I have found there is karmic cleansing in a
rainstorm… if you so choose.
    And I do.
    So, I find myself
        stripping my shirt
        and losing my shoes.

Barefoot and bare-chested,
    I expose my skin and
        my soul
        to the downpour,
        washing away
        the troubles
        that have tested
        my strength and patience.

Words After Waking

This troubled piece of me:
        I do not scorn,
        but it calls to be released.
        So, I kneel with the rain,
        and I mourn.

As I rest here on my knees,
something catches my attention –
It's the presence of the Trees.
They witness my process and meditation.
A gentle reminder that
        Mother's precipitation is a
        potent medication.
Silent observers of the world, ancient and wise.
They stand with me as
 Her remedy works,
        and I rise.

And even though storms may seem somber,
I can't help but ponder
        what good things will come
        from this weather
        we should not squander.
My mind knows there is something
less obvious
        behind those
        lightning shows.

And this is a meditation,
so frankly… anything goes.

Part III

And unlike my mind,
        this storm has its limits.
        This too shall pass.
                It's just a matter of minutes.
        Maybe hours.
        Or days.
        Possibly even years.
But in due time,
I'll ride this out, and
my storm clouds
will clear.

Maybe that's the appeal that draws me in.
This storm is a reminder that
        even when things are
        dark, loud, and scary,
                embracing the moment
                for all that it's worth
                is necessary.
Like fuel for the spirit
        to help me carry
        the weight of this
                extraordinary
                human condition.
The occasional storm could be the
very thing required to
        elevate my conscience to
        the next level higher and
                transcend the ailments that
                have plagued me prior.

This feels like the deeper reason.

Words After Waking

And it hit me when the sun broke through:
I just rode out an entire thunderstorm waiting for you.
But I recognize this storm was
>*mine and*
>*mine alone.*
And I'll keep on waiting as you weather your own.
With each storm that passes,
>*we will notice the*
>*trust that we have grown,*
>*as I patiently wait for*
>*the last one we weather alone.*

Here is my suggestion, friend:

Sit in the rain next time you get the chance.
And if you have it in your spirit,
> maybe even dance.

This treatment is proven to
clear your mind and
> strengthen your stance.

Do it alone or do it together.
Just don't waste this beautiful weather.

Part III

INTERIM

June 2023

I was playing chess with a good friend recently.
She advanced her knight,
watched as I examined the board,
then asked me:
>"How is your heart?"

That's a great question.
Asked with genuine care and curiosity.
The most meaningful kind.
I'm glad she asked.
I get to share with her an intimate piece of my mind.

I take pause and smile.
My thoughts need a moment to compile...
because there are many.
"Heavy" I answer,
with brevity.
Because even though it is whole by itself,
>it calls for my Other
>who knows they are ready
>for the lifelong commitment of
>love and longevity.

She nods.
She knew my answer before asking.
With her, it's a futile effort to keep my heart in disguise
>because this friend sees me with
>much more than just her eyes.

Words After Waking

And she follows up with another:
"How do you manage to balance such a weight?"
"Trust."
It's a tall order to stand patiently at the ready,
But I do what I must.

This balance is an oscillation between
eagerness for the union to be and
reverence for the process of becoming.

Of course,
it would be nice if my person were here
      to join me on my daily stroll,
      but it's worth the wait
      to be joined at the soul.

And this waiting game wouldn't be so tough
if my person felt further away but,
what presents a challenge
for this balance
is that she feels so close!

Like we are breathing the same air
Like I could open my hand and feel her there.
Like I could embrace her and smell her hair.
Like this energy we feel is a rare thing we share.
Like the anticipation is almost too much to bear.
Like she's sitting across from me in that chair.
Like she's the one asking me meaningful
      questions spoken with care.

Part III

No, I'm not confused.
I'm simply
> waiting for
> her to choose
> to be my muse.

But in this interim, I'll wait. I have enough to keep me growing and occupy my plate.
And when she's ready,
> she'll meet me at the table
> to share with me the life
> she wants us to create.

Words After Waking

Part III

MOTHER'S LOVE

May 2023

In your unique way,

Show Mother that you love Her.

She shows you daily.

Words After Waking

Part III

UNTITLED #2

Amidst the noise,

hold space for

the sound of silence

Words After Waking

Part III

DEAR YIN

August 2023

Dear Yin,

There is something I need to get off my chest.
I've thought through as much as I could
and felt through the rest.
You taught me that.

It's been an honor becoming familiar these past few years.
You taught me many things I needed to learn that I now hold dear.

Things like:
It's okay to be afraid.
It's okay to be sad.
It's okay if I misplayed my hand and
It's okay to be mad, and disappointed in myself.
It's okay to feel the shame, shed the tears, and
      accept the help.

With unconditionally open arms, you embraced me when I entered the Garden with my
      head low and
      spirit broken.
I learned you are always in the background,
      eternal and
      soft-spoken.

Words After Waking

You showed me how to speak my truth and let go of the
notion that kept me from reaching my deepest oceans.
And how to use my
>breath in idle motion
>to guide myself
>with quiet through
>frenzied commotion.

Now – This is not a goodbye letter.
Rather, a love note to my softer side.
Letting you know that I am well
and together in soul, we'll always reside.

We are inseparable – Parts of a whole.
But any more time away from Yang
will keep us from our goal.

So like the best mother, which I see that you are, It's best our time gets placed on the sidebar.

Yes – Your softness is essential and only learned in the
garden, but now takes away from training time to
>harden myself with
>the troops and the tribe
>>so we can all walk tall
>>with safety and pride
>>>and freedom,
>>>keeping our Garden
>>>that of Eden.

Part III

So, I'm sure you understand – The best way to steward the
land is to muddy my hands in the place
        where men fight and brace to
        prove their worth and
                earn their space
                amongst the bruised
                        before returning home
                        from a day well-used.

Yes, I do – I feel myself long
to return to the battleground,
where warriors belong.
Days from here will fill with Yang,
        hearing swords clash
        and weights clang.
                It's time to return to the dirt,
                to lift heavy things,
                and live by the code to
                spread my wings.

I must get back to my nature. Back to climbing the mountain
with its share of danger
        and trouble
        and falling rocks
        and roadblocks.

And rest assured, we will acquire some
        scars and a bruise
        because the life worth living
        has mountain views.

And a lesson for the climb keeps our vision true.
That is: The strongest of us push on and see it through. It doesn't matter how you feel,
> we have a job to do.
>> So square up and return Life's punches
>>> with your own 1-2.
>>> And when knocked down,
>>> don't stay on the floor.
>>> Stand tall and strike back
>>>> with a strong 3-4.

Yin, making footsteps in the garden is comfortable, but if we stay here, we'll perish.
It's time to step back into battle –
both of which, we cherish.

Part IV

"Be the guy that still pushes on and sees it through, even if you don't know how to... yet."

(from Be The Guy)

Part IV

BE THE GUY

September 2023

Lately, things are really coming together for me.
This comes after years of hardships of varying degree.
Finally, I have found myself and balanced my chi.

I realize that all the trials I endured on my personal path had to be faced to ensure that I actually grew from my past.

These lessons shaped the man I am today.
If my friend asked for advice on
        how to handle himself in a way
        that keeps him steadfast,
            so he does not stray
            from the path that
                keeps the wolves away,

I would say:

"Be The Guy.
 Be The Guy."

What I mean is:
Be the guy that keeps the wolves at bay. Someone has to.
Because they never really go away.

Regardless of your standing, you can hold yourself to a standard of conduct that realizes
        truth,
        trust, and
        strength –

Words After Waking

Allowing you to
lead your tribe of
        whatever size
        down a road of
        whatever length.

Being this guy is a tall order.
It's not going to be easy.
It never has been.
It's not supposed to be.

I have learned some things as I've grown.
I'll share some now, so
        take what you like
        and make it your own.

I use these next few rules to keep my spirit high in a world that seems determined to see joy run dry.

This is the code I live by:

When walking, walk upright.
When greeting, shake hands firmly.
When you must speak, speak true.
When deciding, apply discernment.
When searching for meaning, pursue
        responsibility.
Prepare the mind and body for both peace and
        hostility.

Part IV

Subscribe to the ways of resilience and love, minding that
>so below
>as above.

Remember that sentience is the superpower.
Be mindful to both move and feel.
If we become stuck in one,
>we only see half
>of what is real.

And if something as powerful as the oceans
>has tides both
>high and low,
>who are we to stay down
>when delivered a blow
>that floors us?

And we don't exactly know
>how or when
>we will get back up again.

But we know we will.
So be the guy that still
>pushes on and sees it through
>even if you don't know how to... yet.

The Law of Accumulation does wonders in this regard.

If you find posture slumped, relearn to walk tall
There is no need to dwell on any of all
>the mistakes made
>on the path to becoming
>>who and what
>>you are today.

Words After Waking

Share your sage advice with those who ask. To them,
    reveal your truth and
    remove the mask.

In times of distress for you or a friend,
    deliver the truth
    so your fellow man can mend.
Put a hand on
    his shoulder and
    hold strength in your eyes.
Say that it will hurt,
    you should feel it,
    and don't apologize.
We were built to get
    stronger from the
    struggles of our lives.

And lastly:
In your meditations, consult
    Earth,
    Moon,
    Sun, and
    Space.
Their perspective will keep you wise and give you grace.

To sum this all up:
Do hard things.
Cultivate love in all its forms.
Take the time to fully know yourself.
And stay true to what that is.
Because any feeling fully felt –
    That is bliss.

Part IV

FAMILY MEETING

September 2023

Mother Nature.
Father Culture.

If we are brothers and sisters,
I call a family meeting.
There is something I need to say
about what I've been seeing.

I'll make this brief.
I'll try not to cause any more grief
       than necessary.
But staying silent is worse than just
       some stress to carry.
Because frankly, it's our duty to speak up when
       we see a threat or
       something scary.

Mom, you are the source of life itself in the form of heartbeats and weather. You innate power makes you both creative and deadly.
But I don't see you killing me anytime soon.

Dad, on the other hand. I know that you plot and scheme for more power in
       secret rooms.
And I think it's clear to everyone here that your selfish dealings will dead end at
       our early doom.

Now – I know it's our nature is to change through time, but you have changed in a way that steps far out of line.

And I can't speak for Sister, but I will call you out on your recent decline.

The Father I once knew is dead.
And so is the old version of me.
It's time to change the patterns on this family tree

Part IV

UNTITLED #3

The energy of our days will vary.

Some will be light – others heavy.

Learn what you can from them all.

Words After Waking

Part IV

THE PERFECT SHOE

February 2024

Perfectionism is a shoe.
Two sizes too small for any man.

Wearing it is
> painful,
> uncomfortable, and
> binds us to an
> unnatural posture.

And still – A great number of people will
> force themselves
> into a container
> that was
> never made for them.

In a very real sense, it smothers the sole.

We were built to run and move
> with freedom
> enough to
> find our groove.

And when we remove these limiting binds,
> we discover ourselves,
> run free, and
> hit our stride.

It's a powerful thing to
>	leave our
>	perfect shackles
>	behind.

But it seems all too common to push for perfection at some point in our lives.
For some it is forever.
Others, only a short span of time.
And when we do, we walk around
>	for a mile or two
>	only to find
>	these shoes were made
>	for someone who
>	no-one should
>	aspire to.

You don't have to be flawless to be perfectly you.

So, wear the shoes that call to you.
Or form your own and walk tall.
And you can always choose to
>	wear no shoes
>	at all.

Part V

Hold space for her to be the River

and you will be her Stone.

(from Yoni)

Part V

HEART BEATS

February 2025

There is a woman who walks the unbeaten path. She pays close attention to the
> wiggles of the world
> that form a
>> picture-perfect scene of
>> squiggles and curls –

Like her hair
after a night
in braids.

She is the woman who walks the road less traveled.
She spots the ways
> where footprints
> have yet to be laid
>> and insists that
>> she be the one
>> to see them made.

For her, it's about maintaining that sense of wonder in the world. The kind of wonder she remembers as a girl who
> mingled freely
>> among the spirits
>>> of the old mountains.

This woman dances to the beat of her own drummer.
She tried to go along with the crowd, but she felt
> herself smothered.

Words After Waking

She was holding her breath while under the cloud
       of mindless opinions
       from countless others.

And in order to dance, you must be able to breathe.

So how do I know that this woman and I are meant
to be? Because first,
I found my Self.
Then
She found me.

Then, shortly thereafter, we found ourselves dancing to the
exact same beat.
It seems each drummer
       keeps time
              for two hearts
                      to meet.

Part V

YONI

September 2023

The power of God is not found in the skies.
It resides much lower, in fact.
In the portal between her thighs.

She is literally the gateway between worlds.
And one of life's greatest pleasures is
        Loving the God
                I see in her
                        until our
                                toes curl.
And then some.

Genuinely, worship the power of the Yoni.
It gets stronger with light from
your heart and
your wand.

And if handled properly, your life will bloom
beyond what you could imagine on your own.

Hold space for her to be the River
and you will be her Stone.

Words After Waking

Part V

UNTITLED #4

Vulnerability elicits trust and connection.

Choose the person that

Sees your depths and

Dives into your deep.

Words After Waking

Part V

THE LIFE WE EARNED

March 2024

In the mornings we hunt.
Because here,
you eat what you kill.

It's not enough to simply wish for what you want.
You must also have the will
and appropriate effort to see it to fruition.

For now, we live in the city,
but this is not where we will stay.
We will live
in the country with
>   fields and
>   flowers and
>   forests someday.

But this is the place of commerce and expansion.

We must earn our way to our cozy three-bedroom mansion.
We must earn our departure from this concrete madhouse
>   where every other corner
>   stands a too big glass house
>   which seem to be the homes
>   of people who just can't help
>   but throw stones.

But it's not all their fault.

Most city-dwellers are simply programmed this way.

Words After Waking

And this is how we will earn our exit from this place:

We will be a Light in this
        dark spot for the soul
        that shines on the face
        of the collective whole.
We heal people in need in
        our own special way
        and help them remember to
        both work and play
so their family and children do
        not walk through this life
        with wounds of dismay
        in a world full of strife.
We make people strong
        so their souls will not fray
        in the spiritual battleground of
        the city today.

I breathe

Then, we will raise our family away from this place.
We will raise our family where the
        sun kisses our face
        and blesses our skin
as we watch the best chapters
        of our life
        truly begin.

When I close my eyes, I see our home. It has horses past the garden and space to go be.
This is the vision for my family and me:

Part V

The children have room to go play, whether making forts or climbing trees. Not in a yard, no, but a field to be free! Free in this field to just go out and be.

How they play? Doesn't quite matter me.
Run fast or skip or just meander around.
        Or even if they want,
        simply lay down on the ground.
        Or maybe swim in the spring
        below our 2,000-foot mound.

They'll finally come inside from a day consumed by fresh air and dirt that ends in the mud room.
And they'll rush to give mom the bundle of flowers they picked in full bloom.
I like to think they learned that from me.

Our home has a covered patio in front and in back.
It is here we share
        silence and
        tea and
        deep belly laughs.
It is here she notes the beauty in the
        sunsets and sunrise,
while I notice the beauty that lies
        deep in her eyes
as we teach the kids to pray with
        Mother Earth, Moon, and Sky.
We teach them to
        be honest,
        work hard, and
        stay true to yourself.

And that integrity
> and discernment
> will lead to
> spiritual wealth.

In this life, we wish no more.
Because we live on the hill we envisioned years before. We will hold each other and say:
> "It wasn't easy, but we did it.
> We earned the life we adore.
>> I'm with you always and
>> I love you evermore".

Part VI

To work harder, not smarter, we must untangle old thoughts that mangle and block our true path to riches.

(from The Itch to Be Wealthy)

Part VI

ABUNDANCE PRAYER

April 2024

Bless this food and help it nourish my body.
Bless my Self and nourish my soul.
It has been an uphill climb digging out of this hole.

I'm aware that the incline will remain the same,
But I'm ready for a chapter of more luscious terrain.

I'm near the end of my rope and I can see daylight close.
I see that my time has come and it's time I arose.

I will put forth the effort to become all I can be
and remain ready for abundance flowing to me.

Words After Waking

Part VI

THE ITCH TO BE WEALTHY

October 2024

Riches and sobriety make you
        greater than the
        lesser man.
But without courage and love, you'll always be
        lesser than the
        greatest man.

Now – I'm sure I could endure
        the life of a poor man.
But I refuse to settle until I've earned more than
        the bare minimum.
You know – enough to just pay my bills and
        cover the basic needs.
I'll run myself ragged before I live
        broke on my knees.

And this ragged way of running will not be in vain because it is not for ego or personal gain.
My motivation is my
        soon-to-be wife who will
        soon take my name.

She deserves to feel safe and she will be held
in the financial fortress she trusts me to weld.

Of course, I'll work hard, but more importantly, smart.
Minding that all mornings are like Mondays:
        a brand-new fresh start.

Words After Waking

A chance to put my money where my mouth is
        and use the skills I've acquired
        to work myself wisely
        into a modern-day Squire
who earned my acres with calluses on my mind
        and broke free from poor thinking
        that too often bind
        many good men
        to the dust of the grind.

To work smarter, not harder, we must untangle old thoughts
that mangle and block our
        true path to riches.
We must look for new angles to
        scratch these new itches.

And the itch to be wealthy is not a sin, but
        motivation to jump start
        your fire within.
Use it to kick start your disciplined self and
leave your
        old lazy past
                on the very back shelf.

Now if you're young and wealthy, congratulations.
Your job is to keep it and not let up.
But if you're older and tired, I urge you to get up.
When it comes to your wealth, remember this rhyme:
        You are never late.
        You're always
                Right on your time.

Part VI

UNTITLED #5

It's okay to

know that you're enough

and

want to be more

Words After Waking

Part VI

UNTITLED #6

Enjoy the journey and respect your reflection.

The true prize is progress, not perfection.

Words After Waking

Part VI

NEW EARTH FRONTIER

February 2025

What's right for you may be different than my normal, but that doesn't make it wrong. We don't have to do all things the same to know we belong to the same troop - the same tribe.

Because it truly doesn't matter on what side of Earth's mighty oceans you decide to reside. We are Earths loving family, Kin souls on the inside.

Remember this with your brothers and sisters, husbands and wives. Because we co-create this world in which we build our lives.

That being said – there are some things that cannot be tolerated.

At the time of this writing, it's 19 degrees in the great state of Texas. And that is cold as hell here, but not the worst cold to test us.

You see –
You can't fight that 19-degree cold outside,
but you can fight that cold
   that we know likes to hide
   like a wolf in sheep's clothing
     right there behind
     the guise of compassion
     for fellow mankind.

Those few who do harbor this cold are under an ideological spell. And it doesn't take much to poison the well...
The well we all share.

I know this is a sensitive topic; I bring it up because I care.

The fact is: We've had snakes in the grass for decades now and we have a lot to recover from.
It's appalling what they got away with.
Everything they did makes me scoff.
It needs to be
>accounted for,
>said aloud
>and listed off.

I'm going to list some now so if you need to, strap in.
There may still be some with triggers like a hairpin.

You see, these snakes were sneaky with compassionate lies,
>but their tell was bright hair
>and the hate in their eyes.

These snakes found a way to sit in senate seats
>and they even found ways
>to defund the police.

They only vote for laws that cut us down at the knees
>with 300 pages
>so we can't see
>what deals they decree
>for our shiny new cages.

Part VI

They concealed their true motives.
    Especially their
    names and their faces.

They force-fed Black Lives Matter,
    like we didn't know this was true,
    and excluded every other shade of melanin too.
They flew this on flags
    and wore the fist on their shirt
    as they looted local stores down
    to rubble and dirt.
And in the looting and the riots and civil unrest
    people got hurt and died
    at their "mostly safe protest".

Propaganda was so pervasive, that people wore masks
    everywhere; they got brainwashed into fearing
    their own friends and fresh air.
This happened because these political snakes
    coordinated in secret and
    fear-mongered with mandates.
They locked down their sheep
    who they knew couldn't see straight
    from a jab in the arm that padded their pockets
        and legacy media who
        paired with them lockstep.
"Trust the science" they said, and
    lied to their own
    thinking no-one would notice
    and make them atone
    for the sins they committed,
    these true acts of treason.

And silenced the voices that gave people reason
        to question the outlandish
        things being told
        to everyone kept from
        saying goodbye to their old
        mothers and fathers
        who lie gasping for air
        alone in hospital rooms
        forced to be
        left in despair.

Take note: The people censoring speech and using fear to influence have never been the good guys.

The snakes even attacked children, the impressionable few.
They made them think they could be a Him and Her too.
These snakes made fortunes with not a single regard
for kids they
        blatantly,
        purposely,
        unequivocally scarred,
                the trauma in their wake or
                the bodies they marred.

Speaking of fortunes, they took yours with
        inflationary policies and
        money laundering wars.
Now, in their house made of cards,
        there they sit,
        while your dollar is
                taxed to no end
                and worth shit.

Part VI

They made the population fat, sick, and sad
        and told them "Ill-health is normal and
        medicinal nature is bad."
The people lost trust in white coats and found that they had
        to make Nature a staple,
        not a mere passing fad.

They also sold the great lie of Feminism
        and that makes me sick.
        They divided the genders,
        branding masculinity as toxic.
No, actually,
        Men and Women are not the same.
God made us distinctly different.
        Hallow praise be thy name.
        And this different design is for a holy reason:
        we need each other to thrive.
We could live alone,
        but would be
        living muted lives with
        damped meaning and emotions,
        the very things that make us whole.
We weren't meant to bear alone
        this life's
        heavy toll.

With even more propaganda, they tricked women into
thinking that a life at home with the children is oppressive.
To be frank, my wife is the only one I trust to raise
        our kids with
        our message.

The message of love, strength, and truth
> that not all are the same,
> though we are all equal
> in that we get to
> play this game.

And we must play this game
> with the hand we are dealt.

So go do your best
> and the joy that is felt
> at the end of your
> long, hard, well-worn road
> will be directly tied to the
> seeds you have sowed.

So through the valleys and peaks
> of the paths you will tread,
> learn to think for yourself
> so you're not blindly lead
> to the valley of death
> with no end in sight.

Among shadows and darkness,
> you be the light.

Speaking of The Light, we are less than two months after the
> turn of the tides.

The water bearer is here, and
> New Earth has arrived.

This means we usher in this
> worldly transition.

And we set the tone for man's new
> worldly mission.

Part VI

And this world begins with the
>atonement of sins
>from the snakes that pushed us
>to their very end.

And yes, there must now be full accountability to prevent this infiltration from happening again.

I will not forget the things these snakes have done. To be honest, I probably couldn't if I tried.
I mean hell – I grew up in that age.
And now I must guide
>the next generation
>to raise the spiritual vibe
>>of the planet at large
>>because we abide
>>>by the conscious decision
>>>to live as one
>>>humankind.

I know I've said lot so far, so what's the point that I'm making?

The days of weakness are over, it's time to leave evil shaking.

To the Men:
>Honor your God,
>Love your woman, and
>Defend our land of the free.

I'll fight beside you, Brother,
>if you'll fight beside me.

Words After Waking

We will stare down that menace
>who stands at our gate.
The one who
>harbors that cold-blooded hate
>for the beautiful lives
>our liberties make.

We will strike at the core of the resentful beast
>with our weapons
>>of steel and
>>of lead
>>and free speech
>>and truth.

Because we must be
>Wisemen and
>Bad Beastly Brutes.

It's this kind of wise-warrior protection that allows our wives to live without worry and
>water the joys of our lives
>without needing to hurry.

To the Women:
>Keep him accountable to the things
>that he says. Because a man is nothing
>without his word.

Help him balance his
>Lover and Warrior, his
>Magician and King,
>>so he can honor every day
>>your left-handed ring.

And if he builds you a cabin, castle or dome,
>take it upon yourself to make it a home.

Part VI

This, Sisters, is your greatest gift to the earth.
Use your intuition as Goddess of the Hearth.
Encourage him to be the
>Head of the household
>and you be its
>Heart.

When these roles are embraced,
>I believe your
>best life will start.

Why is this important?

Because if every generation has their Great War, ours is a spiritual one. And ongoing.

From this day forward, we stand with our arms at the ready.
We keep our
>heartbeats,
>breath, and
>families
>steady.

This is how we ensure no evil gains clout.
And there will be more evil,
>of this there's no doubt.

Although man's spirit may sometimes wobble,
>it will only
>bend and not break
>because our kids
>we don't coddle.

From this day forward, raise good men not good boys.

Fathers: teach your sons with the
        tools and the toys
        that will harden their skin
        as they learn how to win
        in the trials by fire they
        burn with their boys.

Mothers: instill the skills and the ways
        of the Garden
        and how sometimes
        it's stronger not to
        kill, but to pardon.
 They will thank God for their
        kind mom and strong dad
        as they teach the
        ways of the good fight
        to their strapping young lad.

Now, these are just my suggestions.
Of course, we are all free to live how we please
        because we live where we do.

And this is not a Democracy.
        It's a Republic.
That's a fact and
        it's true.
It's also true that this type of system is great (the best
actually) but it's also quite brittle.
So, we must keep a lookout and keep our heads on a swivel.

Part VI

So far, this freedom we have is ours to lose, if we can keep it.
Let's not forget: our freedom was born of
>great men in old days
>who flew the
>very first version
>of the flag
>that we wave.

And our freedom lives on in the
>home of the brave
>as long as the
>threads of its flag
>do not fray.

Now I'll make this clear
>in case you didn't quite hear
>how to keep our homeland on
>course in this New Earth Frontier

Your freedom is my responsibility. And vice versa.

This means that when
>we do disagree,
>we are BOTH responsible
>for making sure
>we do so peacefully.

Because we, my friends, are the bond that keeps this fragile system from falling.
We are the threads of the flag upon which I am calling.

Words After Waking

The world may think us arrogant
>	because we are proud
>	but I'm not ashamed to say aloud
>	that this is the best place to live
>	and I hope we all know that by now.

I remember as a child, we recited an incantation.
A pledge to live out the promise of our resilient young
nation. Now, I say this in the most American manner.

I do Pledge Allegiance to the
>	Star-Spangled Banner,
>	and to the republic for which it stands,
>	in this country,
>	brothers and sisters hold hands.

One Nation under God,
>	we are indivisible.
>	divided, we fall but
>	together invincible.

This land gives us liberty and justice for all
>	so we can go forth and proser
>	fill our cups and
>	walk tall.

I'll preach this from a stage and the mountain peaks tall
Because this message is meant to be heard by all.
And you can spread the word too. Do it today. Do not stall.
Because this, my good friends, is our New Earthly Call.

In my heart of hearts, I know this is the message we need.
I'll leave you with that.
Until next time – Godspeed.

ACKNOWLEDGMENTS

Firstly, I must thank my muse and love of my life, Savannah. Your very presence and words of affirmation gives me the encouragement to share my authenticity with the world. Every day, I am presented with the opportunity to move toward a more self-actualized expression of myself for our betterment and that of our family to come.

To my mother and father: Cindy and Scott. You blessed me with a wonderful upbringing and instilled the foundation for the stable and heart-centered values that are the undertones of my poems and my life.

To my sister, Whitney: I would not be who I am today without your presence in my life. You have given me the chance to learn the importance of maintaining familial relationships.

To my close friend, client, constructive critic, and confidante, Ryan: Thank you for being a sounding board and helping me hone my art into what it is today. You are a good man, a valuable mentor, and wonderful friend.

To my readers. Without you, my words fall on deaf ears. In a world where our most valuable currency is time and attention, I am truly grateful for yours. I hope these words resonate with you and spark a feeling of positive momentum within yourself. Build on that.

To everyone else I have crossed paths with throughout my journey, I thank you for your presence in my life. Regardless of the nature or duration of our connection, I learned something from you all and the remnants of our time together are in these pages.

ABOUT THE AUTHOR

Colton Hamilton is a poet, storyteller, and advocate for personal and professional well-being. With a Master's in Health Psychology, he specializes in executive performance, organizational wellness, and holistic personal development. His work helps high-performing professionals enhance their physical, mental, and social resilience to achieve sustainable success.

Beyond writing and coaching, Colton finds inspiration in nature, fitness, and the pursuit of self-mastery — elements that shape both his poetry and his philosophy. He currently resides in Dallas, Texas.

Follow Colton for more poetry and insights:
hamiltonnexus.com

www.ingramcontent.com/pod-product-compliance
Lightning Source LLC
Chambersburg PA
CBHW020243010526
44107CB00002B/76